Portraits

FOR FLUTE AND PIANO   John McCabe

GRADES V AND VI

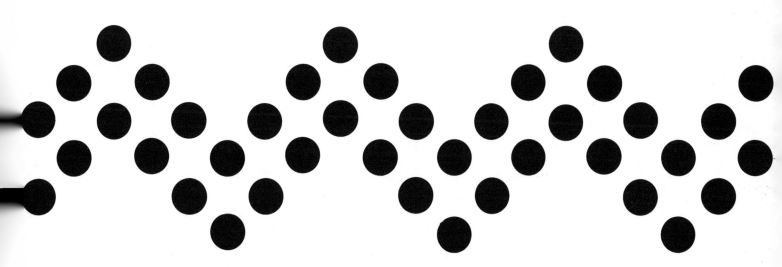

NOVELLO

Order No: NOV 120529

CONTENTS

Total duration 9¾ minutes

Introduction

The gap between starting to learn an instrument and playing 'real' music is a very great deterrent to many players. Consequently, I, and some other composers got together to tackle this problem.

We are producing a series of pieces for many different instruments, playable by musicians with limited technical ability. As a guide, each has a grading similar to those of the Associated Board of the Royal Schools of Music, but I hope people of all grades will enjoy playing them.

Richard Rodney Bennett

Richard Rodney Bennett
Series Editor

COMPOSER'S NOTE

Each of these pieces is in some way a character study or a 'portrait' of some musical style—in several cases the music is a deliberate pastiche or a tribute to some other composer.

The **Gymnopédie** is a tribute to Satie—his own works with this title are perhaps his most popular compositions, and I have adopted the same style for this piece.

Three and Twos started life as a portrait of a Jack-in-the-box—I decided to give it its present title because this emphasizes the rhythmic nature of the music.

Guitar Song is so-called because the original idea of the tune and the harmonies derives from the sound of guitar chords.

Blues—this is self-explanatory!

Vocalise—a pastiche of Rachmaninov's beautiful song *Vocalise*, surely one of the loveliest tunes he ever composed.

March of the Fool—apart from being a March, which emerges from the distance and recedes again, this piece contains a brief reference to the Ballet Music from Holst's opera *The Perfect Fool*.

Scherzo—this is a tribute to a particular kind of composition rather than any one composer. This is the kind of piece so often written by French composers, or those influenced by French music, or by such composers as Hindemith in his lighter mood, and I hope it makes a rousing finish to this collection.

PORTRAITS
for flute and piano
by
JOHN McCABE

1 GYMNOPÉDIE

1' 40"

2 THREES AND TWOS

6

3 GUITAR SONG

In this piece, it is most important that the pedal markings in the piano part should be strictly obeyed.

1' 35"

4 BLUES

Allegro giocoso ♩ = 144

5 VOCALISE

1' 45"

6 MARCH OF THE FOOL*

*This piece is simply a very gradual *cresc.* to *ff* and then a slow *dim.* The dynamics in brackets indicate the progress of the *cresc.* and the *dim.*

7 SCHERZO

Allegro ♩ = up to 144

Printed and bound in Great Britain by
Caligraving Limited Thetford Norfolk

12/96 (26541)

Music for Flute

Solo

Gordon Saunders
Eight Traditional Japanese Pieces
Gordon Saunders has selected and transcribed these pieces for tenor recorder solo or flute from the traditional folk music of Japan.

Trevor Wye
Practice Book for the Flute

Volume 1	TONE
Volume 2	TECHNIQUE
Volume 3	ARTICULATION
Volume 4	INTONATION
Volume 5	BREATHING AND SCALES
Volume 6	ADVANCED PRACTICE

Flute & Piano

Richard Rodney Bennett
Summer Music *Associated Board Grade VII*

Charles Camilleri
Sonata Antica

François Couperin
A Couperin Album *arranged by Trevor Wye*

James Galway
Showpieces
The Magic Flute of James Galway
Two albums, each containing ten favourite pieces by various composers, arranged for flute and piano by James Galway. Both include photographs and a separate flute part.

Michael Hurd
Sonatina

John McCabe
Portraits *Associated Board Grades V & VI*

Jean Philippe Rameau
A Rameau Album *arranged by Trevor Wye*

Eric Satie
A Satie Flute Album *arranged by Trevor Wye*

Gerard Schurmann
Sonatina

Antonio Vivaldi
A Vivaldi Album *arranged by Trevor Wye*